MOUNTAIN STREAM

WEBS OF LIFE

MOUNTAIN STREAM

Paul Fleisher

***B*ENCHMARK *B*OOKS**

MARSHALL CAVENDISH
NEW YORK

The author would like to acknowledge the work of Paul Sieswerda of the New York Aquarium for his careful reading of the manuscript; Jean Krulis for her elegant design work; and Kate Nunn and Kathy Bonomi for their capable editing. He would also like to express deep appreciation for the loving, patient support that his wife, Debra Sims Fleisher, has provided for many years.

Benchmark Books
Marshall Cavendish Corporation
99 White Plains Road
Tarrytown, New York 10591-9001

Illustration by Jean Cassels

Library of Congress Cataloging-in-Publication Data
Fleisher, Paul.
Mountain stream / Paul Fleisher.
  p.   cm.—(Webs of life)
Includes bibliographical references (p.) and index.
Summary: Describes the ecology of mountain streams and how they feed and shelter plants and animals.
ISBN 0-7614-0838-X (lib. bdg.)
1. Stream ecology—Juvenile literature. [1. Stream ecology. 2. Ecology.] I. Title. II. Series: Fleisher, Paul. Webs of life.
QH541.5.S7F58   1999   577.6'4—dc21   97-48279   CIP   AC

Photo research by Ellen Barrett Dudley

Cover photo: The National Audubon Society Collection / Photo Reserachers, Inc. / Adam Jones

The photographs in this book are used by permission and through the courtesy of: *The National Audubon Society Collection / Photo Researchers, Inc.*: Leonard Lee Rue III, 2; Noah Poritz, 12; Hermann Eisenbeiss, 13; Adam Jones, 14; George Ranalli, 16; Gregory G. Dimijian, 20; Stephen Dalton, 21; S. J. Krasemann, 23; Nuridsany et Perennou, 28(left); Gregory K. Scott, 28(right); Sam Fried, 30; Jeff Lepore, 32(right), 33. *Animals Animals / Earth Scenes*: Michael P. Gadomski, 6-7, 15; Richard Day, 8-9, 34-35; John Netherton, 10; Fred Whitehead, 11(left); Ken Cole, 11(right); Breck Kent, 18, 27; Oxford Scientific Films, 19; Ray Richardson, 22; Gregory Brown, 24-25; Raymond A. Mendez, 26(top & bottom); Joe McDonald, 29; Scott W. Smith, 31; Peter Weimann, 32(left).

Printed in Hong Kong

6 5 4 3 2 1

For my friends and colleagues Gregg Neylan, Mary Ann Ready, and Susan Stebbins—strong, innovative educators whose ideas and enthusiasm help me keep my own creative energy alive.

Cool, clear water gurgles musically as it tumbles over a rocky ledge into a quiet pool. A cloud of tiny flies whirls above the water. Ripples spread across the pool as a trout snatches an insect from the surface.

The water that feeds this stream comes from high in the Appalachian Mountains. Rain and melting snow soak into the ground. The water is filtered by the soil as it travels underground. Farther down the mountain, the groundwater trickles out of small springs and forms the beginning of the stream.

The mountains have been here for many millions of years. Their once tall and jagged peaks have been worn smooth by ice and snow, wind and rain.

Even now, water is slowly wearing down the mountain as it carries stones and grains of sand downstream. The stream sorts the stones by size. Where the water tumbles swiftly, it leaves large boulders. Where it flows slowly and gently, pebbles and small sandy beaches are found. The rocks are rounded and smoothed from the water rubbing and banging them against one another.

When we follow the stream down the mountain, we can see a pattern to the water's course. Quiet pools alternate with rocky rapids and waterfalls. It's as if the stream flows down the mountain in a series of steps.

Farther downstream, other springs and streams add more water to the flow. The stream grows wider and stronger.

Each spring, rain and melting snow fill the stream to overflowing. The water roars down the mountain, carrying boulders and tree trunks with it.

In the summer, the stream is shallow and much quieter. Nearby trees use up much of the groundwater before it reaches the streambed. Jumbled piles of dry rocks poke above the water.

WATERFALL

Tiger swallowtail butterflies alight at the water's edge to sip moisture from the damp sand. Chipmunks, wild turkeys, deer, and many other animals from the nearby woods drink at the stream.

In the winter, ice forms on the rocks and along the banks. But even in very cold weather, the motion of the water keeps the stream from freezing completely. Animals can drink here all year long.

TIGER SWALLOWTAILS

WHITE-TAILED DEER

Even in fast-moving streams there are places where the water flows slowly. Behind each large rock in the watercourse, a swirling eddy forms, slowing the currents. The water also slows down whenever it flows over rocks.

Areas of slow-moving water are very important to small animals. Many animals, like this stone fly nymph, have flat bodies that help them cling to the rocks in the stream. Others have claws or hooks for holding on.

STONE FLY NYMPH

WATER STRIDER

Water striders seem to skate across the still water of pools near the stream banks. These insects are covered with a waxy substance that keeps them from getting wet. Their widely spaced legs spread out their light weight. These features let the water striders walk on the water's surface film as they hunt for flies or other insects that have fallen into the stream.

Where the stream is narrow, tall trees arch over it. Moisture-loving sycamores shade the water with their broad leaves. Hickory, ash, and oak trees also take root here, along with many other trees and shrubs.

TREE-LINED STREAM

FERNS

Plants that favor damp soil grow along the edges of the stream. Lacy ferns thrive in shady areas. Rough sedges carpet other parts of the banks.

A thin, brown film of algae covers the stones in the stream. Patches of dark green moss grow on the damp rocks. Like other plants, mosses and algae use air, water, and sunlight to make their own food. Here and there, a few rooted plants like grasses and willows sprout along the wet edges of the stream.

In lakes and ponds much of the food that animals eat is made up of floating algae, called diatoms. But in a stream, the moving water washes diatoms away. Without them, the stream itself can't make enough food for many of the animals that live in it. Instead, the animals get almost all their food from the surrounding land.

Leaves, branches, and other plant matter drop into the water from trees and bushes all year long. In the fall, the stream gets an especially heavy load of leaves.

When a leaf falls into the water, it begins to decay. Microscopic fungi and bacteria digest the leaf. The mixture of decaying leaves, fungi, and bacteria is called detritus (dih TRY tuss). Many stream animals eat detritus.

17

A crayfish crawls cautiously among the rocks, searching for bits of food. It shreds a decaying leaf with its claws. When a crayfish senses danger, it scoots backward by snapping its powerful tail.

Snails cling like suction cups to the rocks. They scrape algae and detritus from the rocks with their rough tongues. Look closely and you'll find the trails they made as they ate their way across the rocks.

CRAYFISH

The caddis fly larva also feeds on algae and detritus. This larva surrounds itself with a case of pebbles and bits of wood held together with sticky silk. The case protects the insect's soft body from most predators, or hunting animals. But trout eat the larvae, protective case and all.

Adult caddis flies live for only a few days or weeks. They stay hidden in nearby plants during the day, and come out in the evening to mate and lay their eggs in the water.

CADDIS FLY LARVA

PLANARIAN

Let's turn over a rock and see what's living underneath. We'll probably find small, arrow-shaped flatworms, called planaria. Their soft, flat bodies cling to the bottom of the rock. Each planarian has two light-sensing eyespots on its head. A planarian feeds on detritus and dead animals. Its mouth is an opening in the center of its underside.

Mayfly larvae, or nymphs, also wriggle under the stone. They live in the stream for several years, feeding on detritus and algae. One warm day the nymphs will change into adult mayflies and fly above the water. The lacy-winged adults live for just one day. They mate, lay their eggs in the stream, and quickly die.

MAYFLY

BANK SWALLOW

Insects and their larvae are a very important part of the stream's food web. Like the mayfly, many insects eat detritus or plants. They, in turn, are food for predators, including fish, frogs, birds, and even other insects.

Swallows and sandpipers eat the flying insects that breed in the stream. Bank swallows build their nests in burrows in the steep banks above the stream. They swoop over the water, catching insects as they fly. When the sun goes down, bats also feast on the swarms of flying insects.

Mayflies are one of the trout's favorite foods. Hungry trout face upstream, on the lookout for insects or bits of floating food. Then, with a sudden swirl, the fish gobbles down its meal.

SPOTTED SANDPIPER

Brook trout have lived in Appalachian streams for hundreds of thousands of years. People have also stocked the mountain streams with rainbow and brown trout for sportfishing.

Trout are active fish that need clean, oxygen-rich water to live. As the stream tumbles over the rocks, air is mixed into the water. Cool water holds more oxygen than warm water, so trout thrive in chilly mountain streams. But if a stream becomes polluted, or the water gets too warm, the trout quickly die.

Trout swim upstream to spawn, or lay their eggs. The female digs a shallow hole in the pebbles with her tail and lays her eggs in it. After the male fertilizes the eggs, she covers them with gravel. When the young trout hatch, they stay hidden in the gravel and live on their yolk sacs for several weeks.

25

SAND SHINERS

MOTTLED SCULPIN

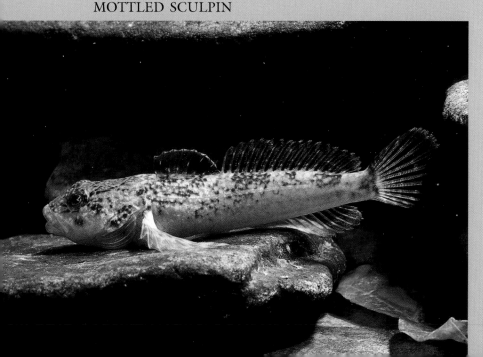

Many animals move upstream at some time in their life cycle. That way, the entire stream is used as a habitat. If animals only traveled down with the current, the upper part of the stream would soon have very little life.

Mayflies and other insects usually fly upstream to mate and lay their eggs. Minnows and other small fish move upstream too. Blacknose dace, shiners, and sculpins dart through the water from one shallow pool to another.

FRESHWATER MUSSELS

Even freshwater mussels move upstream. With the teeth on their shells, the tiny mussel larvae grab onto the gills of a fish and catch a ride upstream. Then they let go and settle to the bottom.

A TADPOLE BECOMES . . . . . . A GREEN FROG

In the spring, green frogs lay their eggs in pools. The jellylike eggs stick together so they won't be washed away. When the eggs hatch, the new tadpoles swim in the water like fish. Later, the tadpoles grow legs and become adult frogs. This change is called metamorphosis (meh tuh MORE fuh siss). Tadpoles feed on algae and detritus, and adult frogs eat insects, worms, and other small animals.

The painted turtle likes slower moving water too. It is cold-blooded, which means it gathers body heat from its surroundings.

Before the turtles go hunting, they warm their bodies by basking in the sun. Painted turtles eat crayfish, insects, worms, and plants.

EASTERN PAINTED TURTLE

A merganser paddles in a quiet pool. The merganser is a diving duck. It gathers snails, insects, and even small fish in its bill as it swims underwater.

HOODED MERGANSER

Another hunting bird, the green heron, stands still in the shallow water. When a fish swims by, the heron snaps it up in its sharp beak.

GREEN HERON

OTTER

MINK

The stream provides food and water for many of the creatures in these mountains. This sleek river otter lives in a burrow hidden in the stream bank. The otter is a powerful swimmer. It swims underwater and catches fish in its sharp teeth. The playful otters like to slither down muddy stream banks into the water. In the winter they even slide on the snow.

Mink follow the waterway, hunting for mice and other small mammals and birds. They, too, are excellent swimmers and often dive into the water to catch crayfish, frogs, and fish.

We might even see a black bear near the stream. Black bears depend on roots, bark, berries, and acorns for most of their food. But they also eat animals, including insects and small mammals. Every now and then they even fish, using their sharp teeth.

BLACK BEAR

We depend on streams too—clean, healthy streams. Flowing streams can clean themselves by washing most harmful pollutants away quickly. But streams that run through human settlements need our protection.

If we treat a stream with care, it will provide food, water, and shelter for a wide web of plant and animal life for many, many years.

STREAM IN WINTER

Can you name the plants and animals along this mountain stream?

Turn the page to check your answers.

Plants and Animals Found Along This Mountain Stream

1. tiger swallowtail	7. white oak	13. brook trout	19. mink
2. chipmunk	8. crayfish	14. rosy-faced shiner	20. black bear
3. wild turkey	9. snail	15. green frog	21. green ash
4. white-tailed deer	10. caddis fly	16. painted turtle	22. sculpin
5. stone fly	11. mayfly	17. green heron	
6. water strider	12. spotted sandpiper	18. river otter	

FIND OUT MORE

Barrett, Norman S. and Jenny Mulherin. *Rivers and Lakes*. Danbury, CT: Franklin Watts, 1990.

Cherry, Lynne A. *A River Ran Wild: An Environmental History*. San Diego, CA: Harcourt Brace, 1992.

Ganeri, Anita. *Rivers, Ponds, and Lakes*. Parsippany, NJ: Dillon Silver Burdett, 1992.

Mariner, Tom. *Rivers*. Tarrytown, NY: Marshall Cavendish, 1990.

INDEX

ABOUT THE AUTHOR

In addition to writing children's books, Paul Fleisher teaches gifted middle school students in Richmond, Virginia. He is often outdoors, fishing on the Chesapeake Bay, walking, or gardening. Fleisher has visited the Blue Ridge Mountains of western Virginia and their clear, tumbling streams many times.

The author is also active in organizations that work for peace and social justice, including the Richmond Peace Education Center and the Virginia Forum.